Losir

C000186156

Peter Arnott was born in Glas
professional playwright with
Glasgow) and *White Rose* ar
in 1985) he has written plays and songs (with Craig Armstrong),
cabaret (with Peter Mullan) as well as the occasional film and TV
script. He worked extensively with Wildcat Theatre Company,
writing, again with Peter Mullan, the Poll Tax musical *Harmony
Row* among others. His work has often had an historical focus,
including *Muir* and *The Wire Garden* along with comedies like
Losing Alec and his versions of modern European classics like
Durrenmatt's *The Visit* and Brecht's *Puntila*. More recently, his
trilogy of classic adaptations for the Citizens' Theatre's multi-
national community company have had great acclaim. His play
The Breathing House won the TMA Award for best new British
play of 2003. His most recent play *Cyprus* was specially
commissioned for Mull Theatre Company and transferred to the
Traflagar Studios in London in December 2005 and tours in
Scotland in 2007. His plays have also appeared in Cork, New
York, Melbourne and Moscow.

fairplay press

Losing Alec

by Peter Arnott

fairplay press

First published by fairplay press, an imprint of Capercaillie Books Limited in 2007.

Registered office 1 Rutland Court, Edinburgh.

© 1988 Peter Arnott. The moral right of the author has been asserted.

Printed by Thomson Litho, East Kilbride.

A catalogue record for this book is available from the British Library.

ISBN 978-0-9551246-3-1

The publisher acknowledges support from the Scottish Arts Council towards the publication of this title.

 Scottish **Arts** Council

Introduction

The play is set over a weekend, Friday to Monday, in Glasgow in 1988. In some ways it feels to me to be very specific to that time and place. Alec MacSwiney, the deceased, represented for me a generation whose hopes had gone sour on them, being delivered a *coup de grace* in the era of Margaret Thatcher, which seemed at that moment, after the Tories had won again in 1987 with an increased majority, itself to be interminable as the grave. Scotland, of course, had decisively rejected the Tories, but it made, or seemed to make, absolutely no difference.

Hence the tone of the play. Black hearted futility, a family turning in on itself, having to relinquish one set of values and uncertain as to whether there will ever be any other values worth finding to replace them. Hence also the rather fierce joy of writing Alec himself, the ghost who won't lie down, lashing his survivors with guilt and contempt. The defiant laughter of a dead man.

The other characters, Mae, his widow, his children Tam and Jeannie, his friend Donald, and Tam's ex, Lizzie (who is the only one not haunted . . . hence representing a way back towards life) revolve around this baleful centre. The play was first produced at the Tron Theatre in Glasgow in 1988. If I discovered anything about theatre when I was writing it, and working with the director, Michael Boyd, whose understanding of these things was a lot deeper than mine, it was that the structure of a play has to be predicated on the response of an audience to the forces competing for their attention on the stage. The audience *liked* Alec – he was funny, and he spoke to their anger and despair. They rather shared his despising attitude towards the living, which included, of course, the audience themselves. Self loathing was something of a *sine qua non* in Scottish culture at the time.

But in Phil McCall's performance as Alec, while agreeing, as he told me he did, with every word Alec said about the namby pamby next generation, he found the real core of Alec's hatred, to be fear and self doubt . . . and when he disappeared through the light flooded door that was still upstage centre of the Tron's stage in those days, it was something of an apotheosis.

As was the *coup de theatre* that Michael had devised for his exit. The stage was hung throughout the show with huge black drapes set to drop at that very moment, and reveal a scaffolding structure on which a soprano sax player called Tim was revealed in a tux, lifting Craig Armstrong's soaring score towards a finally welcoming heaven. Of course, half the time the drapes got stuck and Tim remained anonymous . . . salvation is a provisional stage effect at best.

That show was the first time I'd worked with Craig, and his first dramatic score. He's since gone on to rather grander things with scores for films like *Moulin Rouge* and *World Trade Centre*. It was also the theatre going public's first encounter with Peter Mullan in a comparatively straight role, and my first encounter with Kathryn Howden who played Hannah years later in *The Breathing House*, and one of many collaborations with both Jeanette Foggo and Stewart Preston . . . who played Donald again more than ten years later, requiring less white paint in his beard. Eileen Nicholas as Mae, (again playing an age well beyond her years) was the emotional centre of it all.

I remember it as the most wholly satisfying show that I did in the 80s, and the one that best captured the rather desperate, angry energy of the time. And who was to know, that in Whitehall, even as we rehearsed, Margaret Thatcher was deciding to try out the Poll Tax in Scotland, which she did and so contributed to her own downfall.

In the end, nothing is forever.

Peter Arnott, 2006

Characters

ALEC MACSWINEY: the deceased.

MAE: his widow.

JEANNIE: his beloved daughter.

DONALD: his loving friend.

TAM: his errant son.

LIZZIE: Tam's ex and a friend of the family.

Scene 1

Glasgow 1988. Graveyard. ALEC'S coffin centre stage, the mourners looking on as at the graveside. Stage left, MAE, his widow, arm in arm with JEANNIE, his daughter. Stage left centre, at the head of the coffin, his friend, DONALD, who glances at MAE from time to time. Stage right, his son TAM, and also stage right, but a couple of paces down right of him, LIZZIE, TAM'S ex girlfriend.

DONALD sneezes. Pause. Sneezes again.

MAE: Bless you.

DONALD: (smiles and nods – to himself) Christ I could murder a pint.

TAM: (to himself, directed at the coffin) Hi. Doon there. You. Kin you hear me in there? Can ye. I'm here tae tread you doon pal. I'm here tae *dance*. See by Sunday, by Sunday, right? Nothin'll be left of ye. Nothin. (He looks over at JEANNIE.) Them that'll miss ye should jump in efter ye, by Christ.

DONALD: (to himself) Nae herm in a pint afore the do. There's gonnae be a do, and I could dae wi a pint afore it. Nae disrespect in that. Naebiddy'll *mind*. I mean they'll no be wantin folk aw up at the hoose in a oner, I'd no think.

JEANNIE: (to herself) Everybody should be here. The hale world should be here. (She looks at TAM and LIZZIE.) What's he want bein here, but? What's he want bein here fer? Or her. What dae they want bein here at aw – the pair ae them? (To MAE) Ye aw right, Maw? Maw?

MAE makes no reply. She stares at the coffin

DONALD: (to himself) Pint of Guinness. An mebbe a wee drap

5

of the Irish would be nice. Just a wee nip. Just fer the taste. Tae mind me ae you.

TAM half turns, holds his hand out. LIZZIE steps up to take it.

TAM: Hiya, pet.

LIZZIE: Hiya. **(She kisses his cheek.)** Ye all right?

TAM: Naw. Garbage.

LIZZIE: Aye.

She hugs his arm.

TAM: It's no real, ye know? He's no left me yet. I still hate 'im.

LIZZIE: **(weary)** Uch, Tam.

TAM: Aye well. **(Pause.)** Costs ye, aw ae this ye know. The broo just covers the buryin'. He'd no paid up his insurance, ur nothin. Aye. We'll forever have the debt tae mind us of ma Da. Am ah talking tae masel or whit?

LIZZIE: Aye. Ye are. I'm no feelin like talkin' tae ye. It's too cold and I'm gaspin for a fag.

TAM: Huv wan then, aye why not.

LIZZIE looks at him.

MAE lowers her eyes. JEANNIE takes her hand. MAE flinches slightly.

TAM: I maybe should've sat up wi im. The other night. In the hospital. I mebbe should've been there. Tae watch. Tae make sure ae' im. Struck a match aff his coupon. Or somethin'. Aye, or I should've wrapped the auld bugger in a bin bag and sellt him aff for research. Or stuffed him, mebbe. Stuck him in the People's Palace like a piece ae old Scotland. That would've been the restin place fur him. But ah wisnae there. Was I? So I'm just no happy he's deid yet. Ye know what I'm saying?

LIZZIE looks away.

JEANNIE: **(to DONALD)** Did ye see the card the Riordans sent. All the way fae Adelaide. And the Johnstones. Fae Winnipeg. Aw that way.

DONALD: Aul Charlie Riordan, eh? Daein well, aul Charlie. Is he?

JEANNIE: Think so, uh huh. Got grandweans oot there noo.

DONALD: Aye. I thought about emigrating. At one time.

JEANNIE: Aye?

DONALD: Funny how there's no merr folk here. Ye'd think there'd be merr folk here. I'm surprised aboot that.

JEANNIE: Aye. It's funny.

DONALD: Why's that, d'ye think?

JEANNIE: I'm sure I don't know, Uncle Donald.

DONALD: **(fondly)** 'Uncle Donald'.

JEANNIE smiles tightly.

DONALD: I thought I'd maybe catch up wi ye a wee bit later up at the hoose. **(To MAE.)** If that's OK. Mae?

MAE does not respond.

JEANNIE: That's fine, Uncle Donald, ye'll be merr than welcome.

DONALD: Aye, then.

Shakes hands with JEANNIE. He moves to the exit before turning for a last look.

JEANNIE: **(to MAE)** Good to know there was someb'dy from the old days stuck by him, int it ma? It's awful important don't you think. Ah think it's important.

DONALD**: (as he exits, turns to think. To himself)** Did I like him? **(Considers.)** Uch. Dinna be daft. Course I did.

He turns and walks to exit. JEANNIE hugs MAE, who is staring intently at the coffin.

JEANNIE: Getting a bit cold, hint it, Ma? We maybe ought to think about getting to the car. Getting on as well. Ye alright, Ma? Ma?

MAE: **(snaps)** I'm alright. **(Turns to her.)** Can ye no see I'm no cryin'? I'm alright**. (JEANNIE stares at her, trembles and breaks down.)** Yer okay, pet, I'm sorry. Jeannie. **(She nods TAM over. He comes. LIZZIE stays.)** We'll get into the car, eh? You go wi yer sister.

TAM glances back at LIZZIE. Then leads JEANNIE to the exit. They go out.

LIZZIE crosses to MAE.

LIZZIE: I'm sorry for yer loss, Mrs MacSwiney.

MAE: Aye. It was good of ye tae come. Good tae see ye again. On ye go. **(They both smile. LIZZIE heads for exit. MAE turns immediately to coffin.)** God forgive me. If I was gonnae say something, ye'd think it would be now I'd be sayin' it, wouldn't ye? But I cannae think ae a thing I want tae say.

She crosses herself, looks for a minute. Turns on her heel and goes.

Pause.

The coffin lid is kicked off with a bang. ALEC sits up, wearing the makeup of the dead, tearing the stopping from his mouth.

ALEC: Holy suffrin' Christ. I'm bunged up like a beer keg and I'm aw basterin skelfs! Jesus Mary and Joseph! **(He looks at the coffin.)** Will ye look at this piece ae nonsense? The Co-operative has gaun tae the dugs. But I . . . am still here. Alec MacSwiney. Late of this parish, unable tae rest in peace. Fer why? *Fer dods ae wud up the arse.* That's why. **(He climbs from his grave.)** Where's the respect, eh? Where's the affection? That's the trouble, that was always the trouble. I slaved for youse bastards, I struggled fer you aw my life, and ma coffin's basterin plywood. There's nae justice, and a Scotsman cannae sleep wi nae justice. **(He starts to exercise.)** Exercise, every day, twice a day, forty seven years. Sixty-four, spry as paint, and ye get hit wi a Morris Minor. *A Morris fuckin Minor.* But I'm rose again, like Lazarus, and fit for it, by God. Haun picked fae the grun. **(He looks at where MAE has gone.)** Couldnae think ae anythin tae say, could ye no? Couldae wait tae be rid ae me. Well, I'm back, bugger ye. And ye'll find I'm no sae easy tae shift. Not Auld Alec MacSwiney. Morris Minor, my arse.

Scene 2

MacSwiney's flat. The stage has a balcony above the mainstage representing the landing outside the MacSwiney's flat, and can be used when more than one location is needed at the same time in addition to the 'balcony scenes'.

The MacSwiney's front room. TAM, MAE, JEANNIE, DONALD, LIZZIE.

TAM: Ye want another drink, DONALD.

DONALD: Well, aye. I will.

TAM: Anyone else?

JEANNIE: No. Thanks.

MAE: Aye. **(To JEANNIE)** It'll be okay, pet, won't it? If I skip ma dose tonight? So's I can have a wee drink. What d'ye think?

TAM: Ye takin somethin, Ma?

MAE: Nothin very strong. Ye know.

TAM: Aye. Well, ye sure then?

MAE: It'll work out all being the same, won't it. **(To JEANNIE.)** That no right?

JEANNIE: I don't know, Mum.

TAM: Ye do want to be careful, Ma, wi they things.

MAE: I'm no long on them, sweetheart, I'll be fine.

TAM pours the drink.

DONALD: And what's London like these days?

TAM: I'm no actually in London, Donald. I stay in Bournemouth.

DONALD: Down at the seaside, eh? Ye likin it doon there.

JEANNIE: Ye had a girlfriend doon there, didn't ye?

TAM: **(glancing at LIZZIE)** It's OK, Donald. It's like Millport wi good clothes on.

JEANNIE: So, what exactly are ye doin nowadays?

TAM: This and that. I was a bouncer for a while.

LIZZIE: You were?

TAM: Aye.

LIZZIE: What beatin up old grannies?

TAM: Skin heads mostly. Oh aye. Ye'd be surprized. **(Shrugs.)** Work in the market there now.

JEANNIE: So what's your plans, then. I mean, it cannae be the season still doon there.

TAM: Yer right enough.

DONALD: I think ye should come home, son. Mae. Sure he should.

TAM: Should I?

MAE: Whatever ye like, son.

TAM: We'll see, eh.

He sits beside LIZZIE.

JEANNIE: Aye, well, there's markets up here as well.

LIZZIE: There's merr than markets.

JEANNIE: Oh, aye, there's shops as well. It's just if yer no qualified, Tam, if ye havenae got *experience* . . . yer not so young anymore . . .

TAM: So I'll just drap deed noo, shall I? Would ye like that?

JEANNIE: What kind of thing is that to say? Today of all days!

TAM: Ye mean ye'd no rather it was me doon in that box?

MAE: Tam. That's enough. If ye've nothing helpful to say ye shouldnae say anything.

TAM: I came, didn't I? I didn't have to.

JEANNIE: I still don't know why you did.

TAM: Nor do I. Welcome fucking home.

TAM leaves the room.

JEANNIE: Well, I don't think that was necessary.

DONALD: Is he alright.

LIZZIE: He'll be fine.

MAE: Ye don't want to discourage him.

JEANNIE: It's the truth. It's no so easy tae hold onto a job, much less get a good one. If ye've let yersel drift the way he has.

LIZZIE: He knows that, Jeannie.

JEANNIE: I don't know what he knows. I don't understand anything he gets himself into.

Pause.

DONALD: D'ye think Tam would fancy the game tomorrow, Mae?

MAE: Aye. Perhaps he would. That's a good idea, Donald.

DONALD: **(solicitously)** And what about you, Mae? What dae you fancy doin'?

JEANNIE: That's right, let's see what everybody fancies doin.

MAE: Plenty time, Donald.

JEANNIE: Naw, Ma, naw. Life goes on.

After a pause.

MAE: Is there anybody who'd like another cup of tea?

LIZZIE: Let me, Mrs McSwiney.

MAE: No, love. Not fer me. I'm awful tired. I'll need tae get to ma bed. I was thinkin maybe for Donald or Thomas . . .

LIZZIE: I'll get ye one up there, then. Jeannie?

JEANNIE: I'll get it.

LIZZIE: I'm happy . . .

JEANNIE: Yes, I know. I'll get it.

MAE: Ta, love. On ye go. That'd be nice.

JEANNIE doesn't move.

LIZZIE: I'll need to be off masel.

MAE: Naw, naw. You stay up here a while. Tam'll want tae talk tae ye. Ye'll no have had a chance.

LIZZIE: Naw. Right enough.

MAE: What about you, Donald? Don't feel ye have tae rush.

DONALD: Uch, no. I'll be heading off once I've finished this one. Old bones.

MAE: It's good of ye. Donald.

DONALD: Uch. I thought maybe I might come over on the Sunday.

MAE: Aye. Come for yer dinner. Ye'll go tae mass on Sunday? They'll be speakin for him.

DONALD: Aye. Aye, I'll do that.

MAE: I'll be up the stair, then.

DONALD: Right ye are.

MAE: Stay still. Have yer drink.

DONALD: Sunday, then.

MAE: Aye. Night, Lizzie.

LIZZIE: Night.

JEANNIE: I'll make your tea.

MAE exits, DONALD looking after. LIZZIE looks at him.

DONALD: **(to JEANNIE)** She's some woman. Your mother.

JEANNIE: Yes.

LIZZIE: Aye. She is.

DONALD: He was an awful lucky man that way.

JEANNIE says nothing.

LIZZIE: I suppose he was.

DONALD: Oh, aye. She's a tower a strength. That's what ye
need, in this world. An anchor. And a wee star tae steer by.
Like Mae. Like yer mother. He was a lucky man.

JEANNIE: Aye. . .well. The tea willnae make itsel.

She exits.

DONALD: See if he hadnae met her first . . . Mae . . .

LIZZIE: Did you know her as well, back then?

DONALD: Well no, no really. I'm just sayin. She was . . .

LIZZIE: Uh huh.

DONALD: Was your hair not longer at one time.

LIZZIE: Aye. Then when ah wis a bairn it was kinda short.

DONALD: I'd best be saying good night to Jeannie and yer man
oot there . . .

Rises, starts to exit.

LIZZIE: Aye, sure.

DONALD: No tae worry.

LIZZIE: I'm not worried.

DONALD: No. Yer right. We dae what we can, eh? It's usually good enough.

LIZZIE: Good night.

DONALD: Aye.

LIZZIE: God help me. They're aw doon there wi him. Fightin yin another fer lack of room. And here's me, right doon wi them anaw. God help me.

Scene 3

The Balcony Landing. TAM smokes, leaning out.

TAM: What dae ye dae, eh? In all decency, what is it ye dae? When the sound ae his voice on the stair used tae turn yer guts tae cabbage, when he made ye miss yer sleep when he came in drunk or sober. When he sent ye runnin, hitchin doon tae London. At seventeen, twenty, twenty-one and twenty four, and the last time, Christ ye meant it when ye swore ye'd never come back. When all ye ever did for him was hate him. Ye come back. That's what ye dae. Then ye spit on his grave.

Enter DONALD and JEANNIE.

DONALD: So this is where ye are, son.

TAM: Aye. This is me. That you on yer way, then.

DONALD: Aye. Listen, I had a thought. D'ye want to go to the game the morra?

TAM: What Parkheid?

DONALD: Aye, what'd'ye think?

TAM: Aye. Why no. Sure.

DONALD: Meet us at two then. *Hielan Jessie's*. Ye mind where that is?

TAM: Oh aye. I think I'll find it.

DONALD: Jeannie gied us a lucky bag.

TAM: Too right. There was me aw morning spriedin pieces. Wir gonnae die of Flora poisoning. **(TAM shakes his hand.)** Thanks for comin anyway.

JEANNIE: Thanks, Uncle Donald.

DONALD: Uch, c'mere. **(He hugs her. She sobs.)** Here noo. None ae that. You be strong for yer mother. You as well, Tam.

TAM awkwardly joins them, and puts arm round JEANNIE.

DONALD: Any bother ataw. Yer no tae hesitate the pair of ye, ye hear me. I'll see ye both on Sunday, and I'll see you the morra. OK, Tam? Best a luck, then, eh?

DONALD exits, JEANNIE pulls away from TAM.

TAM: Christ can we no try?

JEANNIE: Try what?

TAM: Gettin oan.

JEANNIE: Ye mean like tae help each other oot. With ma Ma?

TAM: Aye, of course.

JEANNIE: Course nothin. You wouldn't know where to start.

ALEC emerges. Watches.

TAM: You could help me, ye thought ae that? Ye could stop spittin when I walk in tae a room.

JEANNIE: Well, yer aw growed up noo, son.

TAM: Jeannie . . .

JEANNIE: Gonnae comfort me now, is that it?

TAM: What'll I dae? Fling masel? Ye gonnae poison ma tea?

He grabs her arm.

JEANNIE: Let go.

TAM: Go? Christ aye, I'm intae that. But I'm yer brother and yer stuck wi us.

JEANNIE: Are we stuck wi her as well?

TAM: You leave Lizzie out of this.

JEANNIE: Out of what?

TAM: What ye think of me.

JEANNIE: Aye, well you think what ye like. Yer kiddin no one. Ye'll dae just what ye like. Just like always. Don't you kid me on ye give a damn about anybody else.

TAM: Yer a hard bitch, aren't ye?

JEANNIE: Someone's got to be. We cannae all run away.

TAM: See you, yer merr like Mother Teresa every day. I think the Pope should hear about you before ye rise to heaven. You are getting fuckin worse.

JEANNIE: I don't hurt people.

TAM: Yer bein' modest.

JEANNIE: Like you hurt Ma. Like you hurt ma Da.

TAM: Naw? Yer right. I'm a piece a shite. Ahm no even worth talkin aboot.

JEANNIE: Go and talk tae yer slut in there. Maybe she'll find you impressive. Make yourself useful, why don't ye. Get these doon the midden.

TAM: What? Is naebiddy wantin pieces?

JEANNIE: Naebiddy came, did they.

TAM: Cos naebiddy was asked. They were expected. Fer ma Da . . . the big man. The hero of the people. Where's the crowds, then, where's the weepin and wailin. Jeannie . . . ?

JEANNIE: Ya wee prick. You're nothin tae what he was.

TAM: Christ, nice tae see wer family is still proud. Still deludin oorsels.

JEANNIE: What's oor family got to do with you? You left.

She exits. TAM turns out, yells back.

TAM: I didnae feel exactly wanted at that particular moment. I hadnae realized yez were all sae anxious tae have me around. Bitch. Jesus Christ. **(He considers.)** Chuck the bin bags in the street. Eh? Chuck ma body on the pavement, how would that be? Naw. It's only four floors. Be tricky gettin the hied right doon. I'll no have her feedin me soup in a wheelchair. Be too far up her alley, so it would. So take the bin bags tae the midden, and fuck's sake get tae grips.

He exits.

ALEC: Should've jumped, ya plonker. Saved yersel another forty years of embarrassment. **(He looks into the audience.)** Amazin how bein died can tune yer eyes up. I can see this place in the dark. Oh aye, dead right. The hale scheme. Wan ae the first families in here. They were fightin tae get in. Shangri-la wi central heating. Christ aye. Socialism was respected back in they days. Now look. It's a safari park wi Social Work for keepers. It's only the animals get out at night, and the rest ae us stay on the bus. Well I tellt ye the ungrateful wee bastards would send the place to hell. I tellt ye and I tellt ye, and naebiddy would listen. Well ye'll listen now that I'm a vampire. Near enough. What happened, eh? Tae the decent folk. The ordinary decent folk, the respectable working class who fought for this, and worked for this? Would they have let it get like this? Naw. It was the weaklings, the degenerates, the pampered forgetful wee plonkers who'd nae notion how we suffered, who didnae gie a monkeys for all wer sacrifices, it was them who ran wild, them that turned intae dope-sucking nancy boys, the minute ye tellt them there was nae merr sin. Nae merr sin? Ye'll be sayin next it never rains in Newton Mearns. Oh but we have to be tolerant, don't we, let the wee nyaffs express themselves, find out their ain dirty wee feelings. Bollocks. Decency has risen from the grave. And there will be hell to pay.

Scene 4

Front Room. TAM joins LIZZIE on the sofa.

TAM: Ye all right?

LIZZIE: I'm mebbe bit out of it. And you?

TAM: Aye, aye. I thought I might top masel oot there, but ma bottle crashed, ye know. **(He picks up bottle.)** Ye want one?

LIZZIE: Aye. Wee one.

He pours.

LIZZIE: That's too much.

TAM: Ye no keeping me company?

LIZZIE: Kinda depends on where yer gaun.

TAM: Away. Tae get some distance. Are ye comin?

LIZZIE: Still depends on where yer gaun.

TAM: Nae mercy oor Lizzie.

LIZZIE: Mebbe not. Mebbe I've got better things tae do. With ma mercy.

TAM: I always knew I could talk tae ye, ye know. Ye always made us feel I could talk.

LIZZIE: Sure it's no the whisky?

TAM: No it's not. Forget it.

LIZZIE: Mebbe it's just no the right time to talk.

TAM: About us, ye mean?

LIZZIE: What us? I don't want to talk about us. There's no an us tae talk about.

TAM: Naw. Right enough.

LIZZIE: I came here cos ye asked me. Course ah did. But I didnae come tae talk tae ye. Too much ground to cover. And it's better not to say things when everyone's upset.

TAM: Upset? Cos of ma Da? Had tae happen sooner or later. I hardly saw him for four year.

LIZZIE: I know . . . still . . .

TAM: Look it's no gonnae stop the traffic noo there's nae Alec MacSwiney. No matter what he thought.

ALEC enters, listening.

LIZZIE: At least your father tried tae dae somethin' wi his life.

TAM: Oh aye. The Union and stuff, the Labour Party. But see once it wasnae him up on a platform any more, forget about it. He wasnae interested, and naebiddy was interested in him. Poor aul sod. Ye should've heard aw the things he used tae tell us. I mean, he used tae scare the shite and stuffin out of me by tellin me how important I had to be cos he was my Daddy. No me, ye understand, not who I was. He was important. And he was nothin. He *knew* he was nothin. The only traffic that ma Daddy ever stopped was a green Morris Minor wi a Liberal sticker in the windae. He knew. He was just a wee guy. A wee pathetic lying guy.

LIZZIE: **(ironic)** So yer no upset he's died?

TAM: He's ma Da. Ma Ma's shattered. Int she no. Aye, well that's a poser for me anaw, cos he was just the same wi her. Sometimes . . . when I was a kid, I used tae hope he'd die. I thought that she'd be happy if he did.

ALEC exits.

LIZZIE: Mebbe she loved him. Your Ma.

TAM shrugs.

TAM: Thanks for coming. I might have gone mental. Get ye home, shall I?

LIZZIE: Tam, cmaun. You should stay here the night. Come and see me tomorrow dinner time if ye like.

TAM: At yer work?

LIZZIE: Aye.

TAM: Need tae dress proper then, will I?

21

LIZZIE: It's no that bad.

She stands. He holds her arm.

TAM: Will ye stay till I'm legless?

Awkwardly, she stays. Fade.

Scene 5

The bedroom. MAE lies on the bed. JEANNIE strokes her hair.

MAE: That them all away?

JEANNIE: Lizzie's still here. I thought aw that wi her and Tam was finished a long time ago.

MAE: Things stay wi ye longer than ye know at the time. Ye find out things like that. Times like this.

JEANNIE: Mebbe.

MAE: It's gonnae take a while tae adjust tae it and how things change for us. I mean, now yer faither's gone, the shock ae it. Gonnae take a while tae settle down. Get used tae it.

JEANNIE: Get used tae it.

MAE: Aye.

JEANNIE: You make it sound like getting used to new chair covers.

MAE: Dae I? Forty two years wi a man, Jeannie. Ye get that close tae 'im ye cannae see him. So you don't know what it is ye've lost when ye lose it. No for a while.

JEANNIE: What don't ye know? I can tell ye all about him.

MAE: I don't know why you're angry, pet.

JEANNIE: Don't ye really?

MAE: No I don't.

JEANNIE: Well. I'm angry that it happened. I'm angry findin out the things I'm findin out, even if I knew it all the time. I'm angry with the shite. The shite that he put up wi. Aw the work he had to do, just tae end wi nothin. Aye, and Tam. I'm angry he's no carin. I'm angry wi ma job and this house and this scheme, and *naebiddy came.* I'm angry naebiddy came.

MAE: Jeannie . . .

JEANNIE: It's no right . . .

MAE: . . .There are things ye cannae help . . .

JEANNIE: Are there so? Ye mean it's fine I lost ma Da, it's all right I'm earnin buttons and he ended up wi nothin. *That's all right?* **(Pause, looks levelly at her mother.)** He was robbed, ma. And he just had to put up wi it. Well, I'll no be robbed. Wir no gonnae be robbed again.

MAE: Jeannie, love . . .

But she sees ALEC, crossing the stage towards her, passing TAM and LIZZIE, and she freezes.

JEANNIE: Things are gonnae be nice, Ma. Gonnae be nice. We're gonnae make this house decent, you and me. We're gonnae pay it off and decorate and aw that. I want aw that. I don't want nothin through that door that isnae wanted. I want the ugly things kept out of here. I want it to be perfect, ma, perfect.

ALEC: Hello Mae.

JEANNIE: Ma?

MAE: You're dead.

JEANNIE: Ma. What is it?

MAE: You're dead.

ALEC: Dead bollocks, where's ma tea? Naw. Jeannie, cannae see me. It's you I've come for.

MAE: What do you want? What do you want?

Enter TAM and LIZZIE.

ALEC: Though come tae think of it, yer mebbe no the only one.

MAE: No. Ye cannae. You're dead, you're dead.

TAM: Ma?

MAE: Go away.

ALEC: You thought you were rid a me? You thought that was the end ae it? You thought you could just pull the plug on me? I've come back for you, bitch.

MAE screams and passes out.

ALEC: Ye know it don't ye. You fuckin know.

TAM: Ma.

JEANNIE: Get out. She just need peace and quiet. You get out.

TAM: Shall I get a doctor.

JEANNIE: Go wi her, go on. Leave us alone.

TAM: Now, look . . .

LIZZIE: Tam. Leave it.

JEANNIE: It's up to me, isn't it. What's it got to do with you?

LIZZIE: Tam. Let's go. Tam. There's no point fighting.

TAM: You tell me what's going on.

JEANNIE: Mum's just tired, that's all.

TAM: She saw him. Didn't she?

JEANNIE: Don't be stupid. You're in the way.

TAM: She saw ma Da.

JEANNIE: She wants *peace*.

LIZZIE: Come on, Tam, we don't want a fight. Get me home.

TAM: Jeannie . . .

JEANNIE: Go on.

TAM: Aw Jesus.

He turns, he and LIZZIE exit.

ALEC: Naw. She's no seeing Jesus yet. There still has to be purgation. For her. Aye, son. And for you. But for the faithful, Jeannie. For the faithful, there can be rewards on earth as well as heaven, and I can already see all the angels smilin. Waitin for us. No long, lassie, till there's justice. And you and me are free.

Alec watches as JEANNIE puts MAE to bed.

Scene 6

Mimesis Bar. **LIZZIE working. TAM sitting with a lager. She passes his table.**

TAM: Gonnae stay still a minute.

LIZZIE: I've got an order.

TAM: Ye've no joined the bloody army.

LIZZIE: I'm workin. I still want a job by tonight.

TAM: Can ye no slow down.

LIZZIE: **(as she exits)** I'll get ye in a minute.

TAM: **(sighs to himself, picks up a menu.)** 'Mimesis — the imitation of life.' Oh, aye. 'We in Mimesis believe that life itself must be an art. The art of living gracefully, with a wide range of cocktails, spirits, continental beers and the finest blends of coffee from all around the world.' Fuck me. **(As LIZZIE passes again.)** What's this aboot?

LIZZIE: What, that? That's Willie's bit a philosophy.

TAM: Uh huh.

LIZZIE: Had tae use his degree for somethin'

TAM: Aye. In my day the middle classes brought their sons up to be Doctors.

LIZZIE: Ye okay?

TAM: Aye, aye. I'm just living away gracefully here. Can ye gie us five minutes. It's not that busy.

LIZZIE: Aye, all right.

TAM: Bring us another lager while yer at it.

LIZZIE: Dae I get tae drink somethin?

TAM: What? Ye allowed?

LIZZIE: Water, soft drinks, but no carbonates.

TAM: Nae farting, then?

LIZZIE: Oh, aye, in here we're cool as fuck.

She exits. ALEC hovers over TAM.

ALEC: How's ma wanderin boy? D'ye get yer hole last night? Yer
no lookin too happy? Didnae get it did ye? What d'ye dae? Play
scrabble? I wouldnae be surprised. Yer radiatin hopelessness.
What, she's no supposed tae notice, or is that how ye dae yer
courting noo. 'Fuck me! I'm pathetic.' So this is you now, is it,
son? Forgettin where ye come fae and payin fifty bob for a pint
a lager? That you thinkin you've *arrived*? We were just too
borin for ye, were we? I'll tell ye this, son. If I'd thought for five
minutes your betrayal was gonnae lead ye somewhere proper,
I'd mebbe no have minded quite as much. But this? Nae spine
tae this, son. Nae spine ataw. **(LIZZIE sits down.)** Ho, son, look
grateful. Her Highness here is daein ye a favour.

TAM: How ye doin?

LIZZIE: I'm okay.

TAM: What's that they're cookin. It's bowfin.

LIZZIE: It's cabbage. **(Points at menu.)** Look, Sauerkraut. It's
healthy.

ALEC: Sauerkraut? Who won the fuckin war, eh?

TAM: Cannae handle the smell a cabbage. Minds me of the
close, back in the Calton. I was only wee, but. But that smell.
Ye don't even remember that, do ye?

LIZZIE: I get that smell sometimes, up ma close.

TAM: I thought that was curry.

LIZZIE: Last night? It was.

TAM: So what about last night?

LIZZIE: What about it? What d'ye want me tae say?

TAM: Well ye werenae exactly friendly, were ye? I wasnae exactly
a house guest. Merr like some kind a tramp in from the rain.

LIZZIE: It was too soon.

TAM: Too soon fer whit, nothin happened.

ALEC: Told ye.

LIZZIE: I didnae mind ye bein there. I just felt hassled, okay? Ye were hasslin me.

TAM: I'm no a stranger, Lizzie. And I didnae hassle ye.

LIZZIE: Didnae hassle me? You are aw fuckin hassle, Tam. Nip nip fuckin nip. Love me, love me, love me. Tam, it's been four years since I've saw ye. It's only four days since ye walked intae this pub.

ALEC: Not what I call a pub. Merr like a hairdressers wi optics. A nightmare wi curtains.

LIZZIE: I nearly had a heart attack. For aw you knew I might have been married.

TAM: Naw. I checked first wi yer mammie.

LIZZIE: Aye, and she had kittens at the sight of ye. She's awriddy offerin tae pay fer yer train fare.

TAM: Well that's fuckin charmin, int it?

LIZZIE: Just don't try and get sudden on me. Don't you think you can just walk in here and change ma life. It might no seem a lot tae you, this job, that wee flat in Langside, but I'm sweatin blood tae hang on tae it.

TAM: Who says ye have tae lose it?

LIZZIE: Tam, ever since ye got back, ye've been tryin to move in.

TAM: Just till I find ma own place. Don't ye trust me?

LIZZIE: Why the hell would I trust ye? You don't even remember, do ye?

TAM: Remember what?

LIZZIE: I was gonnae move in wi you. When ye had that place in

Cessnock, you and Dougie. He was gonnae move oot. I was gonnae move in.

TAM: That was never firmed up.

LIZZIE: Ye just *left*. Ye got haud ae some money wi yer pal fae Paddy's Market, and ye just buggered off. It was yer mammie tellt me where ye were. I took money out ma first student grant tae come doon and see ye in London, and after a week ye decided I wasnae really there.

TAM: So, I made a mistake.

LIZZIE: Aye, and mebbe so did I. Last night.

TAM: Lizzie, c'maun . . . .

LIZZIE: I nearly got bumped fae ma course, ye know that.

TAM: I wasnae even here. And ye got bumped efter yer first year anyway, didn't ye

LIZZIE: That's right, ye werenae here. And so I fuckin did.

TAM: Lizzie, I didnae even know . . . .

LIZZIE: Ye didn't even try tae find out. I might as well have been dead fer aw the notice you've took of me for four years. And now ye walk in here . . . and I'm supposed tae ferget about that. I'm supposed tae come back tae life, like I didnae exist till you showed up? I cannae just be there whenever you need me. Ye should have been there when I needed you.

TAM: So that explains last night?

LIZZIE: Naw, it doesnae. If I'd any sense I'd no have let ye near me, no matter what was happenin at your bit.

TAM: Okay. Yer right. Yer dead right. I've been a bastard. I mebbe am still a bastard. But I'm no the same bastard. I'm an older bastard. I've changed. I was a daft boy. I was a daft boy well intae ma twenties. Okay, I was a bully, I was cruel, I dumped folk, I dumped you. I was hurt tae. I was hurt by tryin tae act like a man.

ALEC: You were whit?

TAM: Ye see, ma Da . . .

ALEC: Fuck, aye. Here we go.

TAM: Ma Da worked so hard tryin tae turn us intae wan thing, that I spent aw my time tryin tae be somethin else. The only way I could get back at him was by fuckin maself up. That's what I thought. See when I lost ma apprenticeship, he was that chuffed I could a hit him. Unemployment. It was like a punishment fae God.

ALEC: So it was, we'd went *slack*. Workers that willnae defend thersels don't deserve tae be defended.

TAM: Tell ye when ah really bugged him? When I was wheelin and dealin and I was making money.

LIZZIE: I know all this . . .

TAM: Listen. I hated it. I was living on my nerves and I was gettin too close tae some nasty people. Oh, nasty people. I was meetin guys whose names I used tae whisper when I was in the gangs. Grown up bastards. That's why the last time I went south, I stayed. I found out that the only way tae live wi those people was tae end up one ae them. And that wasnae me. They were just illegal versions ae ma Da. Heroes. Users. The only difference between the gangsters and ma Da was that the gangsters believed in capitalism.

ALEC: Yer aff yer hied.

TAM: I was livin aw wrang, Lizzie.

ALEC: And now yer livin all right?

TAM: But I'm still tryin tae find out what I really think, who I really am.

ALEC: Oh, Christ, he's dribblin noo, look at him.

TAM: And you know me. Better than anybody else. I'm sorry if I'm hasslin ye, but, I'm still nervous. I'm still no that confident masel.

ALEC: Ye done? Is that yer *sales pitch*. Jesus, if *you* cannae stand the sight ae yersel, why the Hell should *she*?

LIZZIE: A new Tam? I don't know how I'm gonnae deal wi that.

TAM: Better be off. Meeting Donald fer the gemme

LIZZIE: Look. Why don't we meet up tonight. I'm no sayin anythin, but I'd like tae see ye.

TAM: Okay, thanks.

LIZZIE: Aileen. The lassie there. She's havin a party. West End.

TAM: Where d'ye fancy meeting up?

LIZZIE: Toon. St Enoch's?

TAM: Aye. All right. Aboot eight?

LIZZIE: Aye.

TAM: What dae I owe ye?

LIZZIE: Oh, aye. Six fifty.

He hesitates.

LIZZIE: Ye okay?

TAM: Aye aye aye. There ye go. Gonnae gies a kiss?

LIZZIE: See you.

TAM: See me.

They kiss, just lips, hesitantly.

ALEC: Aw puke. See you, see me! Be honest. It's pathetic. The boy sprieds his sowl out like margarine. Tae hand ower his baws like that, tae some nookie profiteer, just tae get his itch scratched. Aye. This family made it's way fae Donegal tae Dennistoun, fae the Depression tae the beaches at Sorento, fae Monte Cassino tae the NHS, and we end up winchin in a wine bar.

She exits. TAM grins like a cat. ALEC applauds.

ALEC: Ther'es a victory for the workin class. Proud of yersel, are ye?

TAM goes for a piss, ALEC does the same.

ALEC: What dae ye call yersel, going through that humiliation, just tae pull a lassie. A man would never gie himsel away tae yon. A man's a boneless mess wi nae pride. **(TAM finishes pissing and exits. ALEC shouts after him.)** Oh, but you don't want to be a man, dae ye. Ye don't have the confidence. And I know why. Your mother gutted ye, didn't she son. She saftened ye. Tellt ye everything ye did was just fine, just as long as it went against me, my principles. I know ye talked about me. The pair of ye. Mother and son conspirin tae make their old man look bad, tae embarrass him, humiliate him. I swallowed razors every time I thought of you, every time I saw what she had made a you. I should have been hard, even if you were ungrateful and impertinent, I should have been hard.

The scene changes around ALEC to the MacSwiney's front room. JEANNIE enters.

ALEC: Ah but Jeannie. There's a different story. A soul too strong to be tempted. Ma one wee warmin coal of truth. Ma hope, ma joy, ma Jeannie. I wasnae wanted in this house. Once they had their things bought and paid for, once the world had slapped me in the face. I was just a lodger. But you had respect, affection. Fer yer auld man. And all that he stood for.

Course aw lassies love their Daddy, that's only right. But you shall be my witness. My inheritor. Don't kid yersel, Jeannie. The strongest fire will never wash them clean. It's up tae us tae turn them intae mud.

Scene 7

JEANNIE sits. MAE enters, in dressing gown, dragging a bin bag.

JEANNIE: Mum, what ye doing? I didn't even know you were up.

MAE: Shouldnae have slept as long as I did.

JEANNIE: What d'ye think you're doing draggin things around. Let me take care of all this. What have you got in here anyway? **(She looks in the bag.)** Clothes, Ma? Ma Dad's clothes.

MAE: Uh huh.

JEANNIE: What's this in aid of?

MAE: Clearing out?

JEANNIE: Clearing *out*.

MAE: Has tae be done sooner or later. I thought we could mebbe take them doon tae the barras, be careful tae gie ourselves time tae go tae two or three places, ye always get a better price that way.

JEANNIE: We're not going anywhere today, Ma.

MAE: Why not?

JEANNIE: After last night . . .

MAE: Last night, last night, I don't know what happened last night, but it's over now, and we have got tae get on with things.

JEANNIE: But ma Dad's clothes Ma?

MAE: Have you got some savings somewhere that I don't know about? If there's going to be three of us stoppin in this hoose . . .

JEANNIE: Ma.

MAE: . . . then we're going to have to be thrifty and we can't afford to be sentimental.

JEANNIE: Ma.

MAE: What?

JEANNIE: There's only the two of us. Tam went with Lizzie last night.

MAE: Well, even so, that doesn't mean he won't stay if he's a mind to, and we're still not exactly . . . we still need all the money we can get.

JEANNIE: Ma, this is what I was afraid of. If you don't take it easy you'll wear oot. Until we can be sure that you're completely well, we shouldnae even discuss that kind of thing.

MAE: It would remind us . . .

JEANNIE: Well, for a few days, that might be no bad thing.

MAE: Jeannie, I'm not sayin I want to just forget about him, but it's the ones of us left I'm thinkin of.

JEANNIE: We'll manage, mum. We don't have to lose his memory tae do that.

MAE: It's just his *clothes*.

JEANNIE: Now, Ma, the best thing to do is for you to sit down, and we'll put the telly on, and have some tea, and we'll have a relaxing afternoon.

MAE: Jeannie. I saw him. I thought I saw yer Da.

JEANNIE: Ye just gied yersel a fright, that's all. It was in your mind. It's not that unusual, mum. That's why there are so many ghost stories.

MAE: It was me? Does that mean I'm going off my head, then?

JEANNIE: Not at all. It just means that you're tired and upset, and your mind's playing tricks on you. You just need to rest.

MAE: Jeannie, I don't feel tired. I feel I should be doing things.

JEANNIE: Will ye trust me, Ma? Will ye take my advice?

MAE: I suppose so. Mebbe yer right.

JEANNIE: Jeannie knows best. Now, have you had your medicine this morning?

MAE: Aye. I took something when I was first up. I felt all panicky, ye know.

JEANNIE: There's no need for that. *I'm* here aren't I?

MAE: Course ye are, pet. Course ye are.

JEANNIE: So you sit tight, and I'll put some tea on.

MAE: Okay.

JEANNIE exits.

MAE: Tea. I suppose it's a reflex.

She goes to bin bag. Looks through it. Pulls a suit part of the way out.

MAE: This suit. I mind buyin this suit. I mind how long it took tae save the coupons. Very well made. Six months ration stamps anyway. We'll be okay. If I pull myself thegither, we'll all be okay. You were nice in this. It was a good choice. Amazin that a suit could last all this time . . . it's awful well made.

ALEC enters. MAE stares at him. Tries to deny to herself he's there.

JEANNIE re-enters.

JEANNIE: Ye feelin better now.

MAE: I'm . . . I'm sorry.

JEANNIE: Uch, Ma, there's nae need tae be sorry . . .

MAE: What?

JEANNIE: I was just mindin. How I used tae look forward tae Saturdays. Right from when I was quite wee. When ma Da was workin. How he used tae sleep late, and I'd come up wi his paper and his breakfast. And then he'd send me or Tam, sometimes, down wi his wee bet, and we'd get back, and he'd talk tae us about what was in the papers. And then he'd ask us about school, and what we'd been up to. D'ye mind? Then you used tae get a wee sleep in the daytime on Saturdays as well. Aye. In the afternoon when Dad and Tam and Donald and me went out tae the football. And we'd all insist on mince round and beans for wer tea, and me and Tam would get tae split a MacEwans can between us. There were good times.

MAE: **(looking at ALEC)** Then it aw started changin didn't it?

JEANNIE: The world changed. We didn't change. My Da didnae change. He was always the same. He was like a rock, Ma. He was like a tree.

MAE: Aye he did. I could see it.

JEANNIE: Well I never noticed anything.

MAE: **(to her and ALEC)** He tried tae hide it. But it was cruel on him, Jeannie, cruel on yer Da. What happened tae him. When they put him on short time at his work, then no time ataw. And the phone stopped ringing . . . folk stopped askin him things. They stopped tellin him things. He wasnae in the know anymore. That hurt him. I can understand why that hurt him.

JEANNIE: That didnae bother him wan bit. 'Makin way for the young blood' that's what he used tae say. He used tae smile . . .

MAE: He couldnae stand it. It made him small.

JEANNIE: Ma! What a thing tae say . . .

MAE: And then it was just you and me gaun out working . . . and then you weren't around any more because of Eric and yer Da and them not getting on. And the way him and Thomas used tae fight whenever we saw him, which wasnae much.

JEANNIE: Aye, Thomas!

MAE: **(developing her idea)** Aye. And it was round then, the first time we ever had the Polis round. For Tam. And it was yer Da that was in, the mornin when they came. I was never sure what hurt yer Da maist. His son been in bother – or him no bein' at his work.

JEANNIE: He was ashamed.

MAE: Of Thomas? Or himself?

JEANNIE I don't know where you're gettin these ideas from.

MAE: Aye. And that was an awful shame. About you and Eric.

JEANNIE: Mum . . .

MAE: It could have all turned out better. It could . . .

JEANNIE: Aye, well, it was Eric that left me, Ma. It wasn't my decision. I never left him, but now I'm quite glad, okay? I got over that a long time ago.

MAE: Did ye?

JEANNIE: Of course I did. Ma, Eric wasnae what I wanted.

MAE: Yer Da never gave him any chance. He wasnae what yer Da wanted.

JEANNIE: That's not true. Why does, why do . . . ma wedding, Ma. My reception. He spent nearly half of his redundancy on that, or did ye forget that.

MAE: Naw, Jeannie. I didnae. I just don't know how Eric was supposed tae compete with it. Wi his grand sacrifice. His big generosity . . .

JEANNIE: Uch. It wasnae like that.

MAE: He was just a boy, just a nice quiet boy. Yer Da . . .

JEANNIE: Is that why you were on his side. On Eric's side? Sometimes I thought you liked him merr than me.

ALEC moves to stand protectively behind JEANNIE.

MAE: I was trying tae be on your side. I thought you loved him. Jeannie. I thought ye loved him. I thought you were gonnae get away . . .

JEANNIE: Get away? What's that supposed tae mean . . .

MAE: Jeannie . . .

JEANNIE: Did you love ma Da? Did ye?

MAE: Jeannie . . . of course I did.

JEANNIE: Did ye?

MAE: Yes!

ALEC : Did ye?

MAE: Of course I did.

ALEC laughs. He and JEANNIE advance on MAE.

JEANNIE: Cos there's times it doesnae seem like it. I mean,

there ye were, all last week, ye were taking everything so calmly, too calmly werent ye?

MAE: What d'ye mean?

JEANNIE: Last night Ma. You were buildin up tae it. You must have been bottlin yer feelings up.

MAE: Buildin up tae what? What was I bottling up?

JEANNIE: I'll tell ye this. You were not being how I expected you tae be.

MAE: Jeannie.

JEANNIE: It was like it wasnae him. It was like it wasnae ma Daddy that ye'd lost. Your husband. It was like we were buryin a stranger. I think ye just realized, ye realized last night . . . what ye lost . . . ye lost the best man . . . the best Daddy . . .

MAE: (approaches her) Jeannie . . .

ALEC: (grabs MAE, unseen by JEANNIE) Get your hooks out of my daughter.

JEANNIE: Did ye love him Ma? Did ye?

MAE: Jeannie, course I did, don't be daft. I loved him.

ALEC: He ho de fuckin ho.

JEANNIE: It 's just sometimes I think . . .

MAE: What?

JEANNIE: I don't know.

ALEC: You know, don't ye? Ye know damn fine. You know what you are.

JEANNIE: Ye okay, Ma?

MAE: Aye.

JEANNIE: Ye've gone white.

MAE: Just feelin a wee bit queasy. That's aw. Mebbe it's the pills or something.

ALEC: Or maybe it's your conscience, ye thought of that?

MAE: No!

MAE rushes to him. He vanishes through the wall.

JEANNIE: Ma?

MAE: What do you want! What do you want!

JEANNIE: We'll just have soup and sandwiches for lunch, eh ? Mebbe go down to the shopping centre later.

MAE: Don't leave me.

JEANNIE: Course not, Ma . . . I'd never do that.

ALEC: **(reappearing)** She will. When she sees the poison in ye. When she sees it comin tae the surface. When she understands what you did to me. When she understands how you betrayed me every day of your rotten, worthless life.

MAE horrified, feels vomit of sheer terror rising and turns away, falls to her knees.

ALEC: Bring it up.

JEANNIE rushes to her.

ALEC: Bring up yer poison.

JEANNIE: Ma. Ma. Hold on.

JEANNIE rushes out.

ALEC: Course, ye know yer guilty. That's why this is happenin. Yer makin a confession. There is no love in you. Just poison.

He picks up her face.

ALEC: Aye. Well you go tae pieces. But yer no puttin splinters in ma daughter. Ye'll no corrupt her. The way ye did ma son. Ye'll no put her on her knees, the way ye did me, the way you are now. You will never have my daughter. I'll see ye dead first.

JEANNIE returns, with a bowl and wet towel.

JEANNIE: Any more, ma.

MAE shakes her head.

ALEC: How long d'ye think she's gonnae take it? How long is ma lassie gonnae mop up your boke? Just cos you wasted your life, why the hell should she waste hers. How long before she puts you away somewhere? **(MAE looks up.)** Yer boy? Is he gonna help ye? I mean, where is he? *Where's that wee shite ye were sae fond ae?* He'll take one look at you and get right tae fuck. Face facts, bitch. You are for Gartnaval or the grave.

MAE: Jeannie . . . she wouldnae dae that.

ALEC: Oh aye, would she no? Look at her. **(As he exits.)** It's up tae you. You either dae yerself in, or she'll have ye sectioned. I owe ye the choice, my dearest heart, just for you kiddin on ye ever gave a damn about me.

He chuckles, pleased. He exits. MAE yells as he goes.

MAE: It's not true. It's not true.

She turns and looks at JEANNIE, who has tears in her eyes.

JEANNIE: Ye feelin better now?

MAE pulls away from her. Her face hardens. Stone.

Scene 8

TAM and DONALD, in *Heilan Jessies*. DONALD in Celtic colours. They've had a couple.

DONALD: Ye say she *saw* yer Da?

TAM: Aye. Think so.

DONALD: Must have been awful distressin.

TAM: Too right, Donald. I used tae wet masel when the old Bastard was alive. But, Jeannie'll have things well in hand.

DONALD: Well you and her have *got* tae stick the gither noo, son.

TAM: Easy tae say. Ye know?

DONALD: Aye. Mebbe. I mean, here's me been living on ma own all this time.

TAM: Uh, huh. How'd that happen anyway?

DONALD: Uch. I just never got all that fired up tae be wi anybody in particular.

TAM: Naw?

DONALD: Naw. No really.

TAM: Aye, well.

DONALD: S' why yer friends mean a lot. Listen, Tam, I don't mean tae pry or nothin, but d'ye mind me askin ye what yer thinkin of doin?

TAM: Naw. I've just nae idea.

DONALD: I mean, yer mother will need all the support she can get.

TAM: Aye, aye, Donald. Course.

DONALD: Sorry.

TAM: Don't be daft. Yer entitled. I mean, I've no been here, have I?

DONALD: Yer still family, son.

TAM: Uh huh? Tell Jeannie.

DONALD: If ye were gonnae stick around . . . here . . . it's yer faither's season ticket. I got the club tae transfer it intae your name.

TAM: Thanks.

DONALD: Something wrong, son?

TAM: I'm no sure he'd a wanted me tae have this. I don't think he thought ae me as 'faithful through and through', ye know?

DONALD: Well. Mebbe he didnae. But there ye go anyway. Yer faither was ma friend for all ma life, Tam. So I feel it's up tae me. If it's up tae anybody. Me and Mae. In our ain different ways, of course. These kinda things. Seein he never made a will.

TAM: Aye, well he was never gonnae die, was he.

DONALD: I'm still shakin. Wi the shock ae it. I thought he'd go on forever. The man was merr alive than anyone I ever met.

TAM: Aye, Donald, sure. You were his pal.

DONALD: You have nae doubts on that, son. Nae doubts.

TAM: Naw, naw. I thought he'd last forever tae. Look, do we have tae talk about him? Donald, he wasnae ma friend. We didnae like each other. There's nae point in me pretendin different.

DONALD: It's no right, son.

TAM: Naw?

DONALD: It's no right a boy should feel that way about his Da.

TAM: Who says I'm sayin it's right? I just dae, okay? So, drop it.

DONALD: He talked to me about you.

TAM: Did he really?

DONALD: Aye, he did. About you and Mae and Jeannie. Ye've no idea how much it hurt him when he thought that you'd turned your back on him, son. And it was me that used tae tell him that ye weren't that bad. That you were just young, and one day ye'd appreciate . . .

TAM: I'd appreciate whit?

DONALD: What he stood for.

TAM: What he stood for? Shall I tell ye what he stood for? He stood for aw the things that made me want tae emigrate, that's what he stood for. I've only got as far as Bournemouth, right, but see if ye could get a bus tae Australia I'd be Waltzin fuckin Matilda. I'm no interested, Donald, in any of what he stood for. It's got nothin tae do wi me.

DONALD: Yer country? Yer history? Yer class?

TAM: That was aw him. Him. Alec MacSwiney. He was ma class. He was my history and my religion and my country and he's dead, so none ae it fuckin matters any more, does it?.

DONALD: Is that all it means tae ye.

TAM: It's all it meant tae him. It was aw hot air. It was aw just him, Donald. He didnae really gie a shite about any of it.

DONALD: I cannae believe I'm hearing this kind of talk fae you, fae . . .

TAM: Alec's boy? What about me? Me, ye know? I'm somebody tae, what's left of me.

DONALD: Me. Aye. That's what you're aw about nowadays. Yer a yuppie, that's what ye are.

TAM: I'm a whit? Dae I look like a yuppie?

DONALD: Ye fuckin talk like one.

TAM: Ye ever met one, Donald?

DONALD: I don't want to, thank you.

TAM: You should get out and about more, Donald. Dae ye know what folk do, nowadays, when they hear your kind a talk. They laugh. They fuckin howl.

DONALD: Me and yer Da . . .

TAM: I know, ye fought in a war, and ye gied us everything we've got. Heard it. Aye, well they came and took it aff us, Donald, like the HP took the fridge. And ye couldnae fuckin stop them.

DONALD: And you think it's funny, don't ye? All that we stood for, you think it's funny.

TAM: Naw. They think it's funny. I think ye made mugs of all the rest ae us. Ye mind aw they Saturdays that you and me and ma Da used tae go tae the fitba? Ye know what he did in the mornings? On Saturday mornins? He educated us. That's what he called it.

DONALD: Ye make it sound like . . .

TAM: Abuse? It was . . .

DONALD: Now, I'll no have that . . . that's . . . yer Da was . . .

ALEC emerges to listen.

TAM: He'd interrogate ma Ma, every Saturday mornin, find out what me and Jeannie had been up tae. Then he'd summon us, one at a time, at dinner time, and he'd tell us exactly what he thought ae us. Half an hour each, every fuckin Saturday. I'd rather he'd hit us wi a bottle. I used tae puke. I used tae wet masel fae fear, every Friday fuckin night. I used tae stand in front ae that bastard, and I'd tremble, and the merr I'd tremble the merr abusive he would get, because I wasnae being a man. From when I was six year old. Six year old. Then I'd get sent on down tae ma Mammie for a sweetie, and I'd get to watch Grandstand, then I'd get taken tae the game wi you. That was my education, Donald. Aye well see the schools were full ae pansies and the church had gone saft so he had tae correct all the bad influences, all the things I wanted, all the things that didnae come fae him. He tried tae stub me oot like the but-end ae a fag, so when I was fifteen, I said fuck off. I said fuck you. And I started staying out on Friday nights. Anywhere I could. It was years till I stopped havin nightmares. So don't you tell me what a great man ma Daddy was.

DONALD: Tam, yer a man yersel noo. There's a lot ae things have made ye what ye are. No just yer Da. I can see that. **(He raises his glass.)** Away the Bhoys, eh?

TAM: Fuck aye. Away the bhoys.

They touch glasses, drink up and exit.

ALEC: Away the Bhoys? Away the *Bhoys*? That was ma season ticket. *Ma season ticket*? Forty two years, man and boy! Ye shoulda gied the bloody thing tae Super Ally. What the bloody hell are you thinkin of, McGuire drinkin wi that spunk stain. Are ye tryin tae get yer youth back? Yer handin oot ma memory like a bag a soor plooms. Lose me? Get on wi oot me? I don't think so. **(Sings as he exits.)** *If ye know yer history . . . it's enough tae make yer heart go oh oh oh oh.*

Scene 9

MAE sits, face hard, unresponsive. Dressed to go out. Enter JEANNIE behind. She contemplates her mother.

MAE: It's getting dark. Jeannie. Jeannie.

JEANNIE: Here, mum.

MAE: What's the time?

JEANNIE: Just gone four.

MAE: Four?

JEANNIE: About ten past.

MAE: Still just have time then. Before they get back. How do I look?

JEANNIE: Fine.

MAE: I mean for goin out?

JEANNIE: Ye want tae go for a wee walk?

MAE shakes her head.

JEANNIE: What?

MAE: You phone fer a cab. We can get a bus back.

JEANNIE: Back fae where?

MAE holds the bin bag of ALEC's clothes.

JEANNIE: Ma, we've been through aw that.

MAE: I've changed ma mind.

JEANNIE: Ma, you should see a doctor before we think ae anythin like that.

MAE: When a doctor tells ye that I've went mad, then ye can

47

ignore me. Not before. Ye hear me? Until a doctor tells ye different you will do what you are told.

JEANNIE: Ma, I've got to be responsible. It's up to me to see that you're okay.

MAE: It's up to *me*. He was my husband. It's up tae me. Are ye gonnae help me or dae I dae it aw masel?

JEANNIE: I just don't think it's right.

MAE: Doesnae matter if it's *right*. It's what we're doin. I'll tie this up. You get our coats and phone a taxi.

JEANNIE exits. MAE kneels by the bin bag, ties it up. Then prays.

MAE: *Our father who art in heaven, hallowd be thy name, thy kingdom come, thy will be done on earth as it is in heaven, give us this day our daily bread and forgive us our trespasses as we forgive those who trespass against us, lead us not into temptation but deliver us from evil. Hail Mary full of grace, the Lord is with thee, blessed art thou amongst women and blessed is the fruit of thy womb, Jesus Holy Mary Mother of God, pray for us sinners now, and at the hour of our death. Amen. Glory be to the Father, to the Son and to the Holy Ghost. Amen.*

JEANNIE: **(Entering, ALEC's arm round her)** Here's yer coat, Ma. We'll need tae go down for the Taxi.

MAE: Okay pet.

She turns. Sees ALEC. Knows she has to walk towards him.

JEANNIE: Ma? I'll wait for ye doonstairs.

She exits.

MAE: **(levelly to ALEC)** I want you tae leave me alone.

ALEC: Ye know what she's done, don't ye? Ye think she spent aw the time ye were blasphemin, on the blower for a hack? You've got an appointment. Wi a psychiatrist, or a psychotherapist, or whatever the hell ye call it. On Monday, she's gonnae make an end of ye. Your daughter. Ma Jeannie, and the guys in white coats.

MAE: No.

ALEC: Nae respect, nae affection. Naebiddy lookin at ye straight. Aye. Everybody telling ye lies. Ye know now don't ye. Ye know exactly what it's like.

Scene 10

TAM and DONALD singing in the street. LIZZIE is working in *Mimesis*.

TAM and DONALD: *When you walk through a storm*
Hold your head up high
And don't be afraid of the dark.
At the end of the storm
There's a golden sky
And the sweet, silver song of the lark.
Walk on through the rain
Walk on through the wind
Though your dreams be tossed and blown
Walk on, walk on
With Hope in your hearts
And you'll never walk alone
You'll never walk alone.

ALEC enters *Mimesis* below. Sits.

TAM: Seven one. Seven one, eh?

DONALD: Aye, son.

TAM: The Bhoys are back.

ALEC: I thought the back four were still awful shakey masel.

DONALD: Look. St Mirren is wan thing. Let's see them take seven aff the Huns.

TAM sings.

TAM: We don't care what the animals say . . . what the hell do we care . . .

DONALD: Is this no the place.

TAM: Would ye care for a wee apeerryteef.

DONALD: Aye. Why no?

They sit.

DONALD: Course. Me and yer Da saw Rome, Paris, Berlin.

TAM: Rothesay. Oh aye.

DONALD: In the war.

ALEC: When we fought for yer freedom.

TAM: Hid they no aw been bombed tae fuck? Just askin.

DONALD: Naw. I mean, Berlin, aye, and Rome a bit, but Paris . . .

TAM: I went tae Paris.

ALEC: Eight weeks basic trainin. Nineteen year old. Stuffed a Mills bomb up a Panzer.

TAM: Couple a year back. Just a short hop fae London, ye know?

Went wi this lassie knew her way aboot the place. It was great. I liked it. Hard on the feet, but. Made me think a Glesga. Aw the parks. How there's parks everywhere, ye know. Aw the things I'd got up tae in the parks.

ALEC: Sniffin glue. Spillin away yer manhood.

DONALD: Dear Green Place, eh?

TAM: Aye. Aye. I suppose so.

DONALD: There's naewhere like it. It's no a place ye can just leave. I found that out. I mean, the war was the first time I'd been away. I mean, that was exciting. Far as yer Da and me were concerned, the world went fae Maryhill tae the Calton, ye know. It changes ye, that kind a thing. Brought a lot back wi us.

TAM: Aye. Right enough.

Enter LIZZIE.

TAM: Heh, Lizzie.

LIZZIE: Aye. Seven one. I heard.

TAM: Don't it make yer heart go . . .

LIZZIE: Naw. Naw it doesnae really. I'm glad yer here.

TAM: I'm glad I am too.

LIZZIE: Naw, it's just yer Mum phoned. She said she was phonin fae the Barras or somewhere, she seemed tae be all right. She just said she was wonderin if you were comin back the night.

TAM: Aw, right. Aye. Just thought we'd drap in here first. Have a quick yin. I was on my way.

LIZZIE: What ye wantin then?

TAM: I'll have a lager.

DONALD: I'll just have a whisky, thanks.

LIZZIE: And I'll have a vodka, and I'll get it, okay. I'm just aboot tae knock off anyway.

She exits.

DONALD: If yer Ma was at the Barras . . .

TAM: Why would she phone, why would she phone here. Efter last night. I hope she's okay.

DONALD: Mebbe she's over it? I mean, what was she like this mornin?

TAM: I don't know. I wasn't there this morning.

DONALD: You wernae?

TAM: No I didn't stay last night, okay? I couldnae handle it.

DONALD: Uch, Thomas . . .

ALEC: There, ye see, he's a faithless wee plonker . . . takes merr than a green and white scarf tae make a decent Tim.

DONALD: Well, when we get up there we'll see what needs doin', won't we?

ALEC: Aye. We'll see. You contemplatin yer future are ye son? Or is it just a bus? Oot ae here. Aye. Why no? What's fer ye here? Guilt, self loathing . . . richly bloody merited self loathing I might add.

Re-enter LIZZIE.

LIZZIE: Here ye go.

TAM: How ye doin.

LIZZIE: I'm okay.

TAM: How did mum sound?

LIZZIE: She was just on for a minute. She seemed okay, quite chirpy.

ALEC: Chirpy my arse, she's hypertensive . . . she's gonnae snap like the wishbone oan last year's turkey . . . you wait and see.

TAM: Good. Look, Lizzie, I think mebbe it might be better if we didnae make anything definite about this evenin.

LIZZIE: What was gonnae be definite about it.

TAM: I mean. I'd better go hame and see if everything's okay.

DONALD smiles.

ALEC: So yer gaun hame, son, ur ye? Ye don't look like the bloody cavalry to me.

LIZZIE: All right. Donald, d'ye mind if we have a word for a minute.

DONALD: Naw. On ye go.

They walk aside.

LIZZIE: I've been thinkin.

TAM: Sounds good.

LIZZIE: It's mebbe best if ye do stay at home tonight. If I mebbe see ye the morra, or something.

TAM: Uh huh?

LIZZIE: I mean, yer no gonnae just disappear, are ye. I need more time. I was foolin masel. Thinkin I could just act like it was okay and see how I felt later.

TAM: Aye.

LIZZIE: I mean. We've got tae be realistic. I know yer havin a hard time, but, that doesnae mean that I should just . . .

TAM: So what ye sayin. Ye don't want tae see me?

LIZZIE: That's a phone number for the party.

TAM: Right.

LIZZIE: Don't you dare. Don't you dare try and make me feel guilty. I'm just tryin tae watch for masel.

TAM: What if I said I was in love wi ye?

LIZZIE: What am I supposed to say to that?

TAM: I dunno.

LIZZIE: If I believed ye . . .

TAM: D'ye think I'm lying?

LIZZIE: I don't know what you're thinkin when you're like this.

TAM: When I'm like whit?

LIZZIE: This . . . fragile.

TAM: I'm fragile?

ALEC mimes breaking a wishbone.

LIZZIE: Yer no sure ae yersel, so ye say big important things like 'I love you' and 'Life is really hard' and stuff, well, you have merr respect for me.

TAM: Are ye chuckin me or whit?

LIZZIE: I'm trying tae bloody talk tae ye. I need some time tae *think*. If you keep pushin at me, I cannae think, and I can't afford that. I care about ye. I want ye tae be all right. And I don't think rushin things is any good for either of us.

TAM: Ye've made yer point.

LIZZIE: Have you taken it? Or are you still thinkin it's either one thing or the other. Yer Da's just died, you've just come home, yer Ma's no well, Christ, go easy on yersel. Yer makin yersel desperate. It's no that desperate.

TAM: Yer a great lassie. But ye don't know. I'll phone ye at the party? You enjoy yersel, aye? Take care.

LIZZIE: Tam . . .

TAM: Whit?

LIZZIE: I'll talk tae ye later.

TAM goes back to the table. Where ALEC is now sitting with DONALD.

TAM: We on our way, then?

DONALD: Aye. Better be off.

TAM: I just want tae go home, now. And sort things out.

DONALD: That's right, son. Yer family comes first.

TAM: Let's just sort out one thing at a time, eh? One thing at a time. And get it right, Maun.

Both exit.

ALEC: One thing at a time? Don't you wish it was that easy bein a man. A good man. A good lover. A good soldier. A good Catholic. A good Socialist. One thing at a time? Ye don't know yer born.

Scene 11

Front room. ALEC sits. JEANNIE enters with bag of messages. MAE following.

JEANNIE: Nobody here, yet, Ma.

MAE enters. Sees ALEC. Steels herself.

JEANNIE: Shall we get the messages put away.

MAE: Aye.

JEANNIE: Well, you get a seat and I'll get the tea on. Ye feelin okay?

MAE: Jeannie. It's important. When Tam gets here, I want us to discuss things. But I don't want to fight.

JEANNIE: No, ma. I don't want to either.

MAE: We're gonnae make a clean start.

JEANNIE: Whatever you say. Shall I get the tea on?

MAE: Aye. On ye go.

JEANNIE exits.

MAE: I know what you are.

ALEC: Dae ye? That mean yer no scared of me?

MAE: No. It doesnae mean that.

ALEC: Doesnae matter then. Does it? What ye know.

MAE: You're not Alec. He's dead.

ALEC: So how dae you . . . account for me?

MAE: I don't know. How do you?

JEANNIE: D'ye fancy sein what's on the telly.

MAE: Let's see what the results were. We'll know what kind of mood the boys are gonnae be in.

JEANNIE re-enters

JEANNIE: Oh, it was seven one.

MAE: Aye. Shame yer Dad missed it.

JEANNIE: Hadn't thought of it like that.

MAE: No. It was just something that mattered to him. I always used tae have tae watch what the score was, just so I'd get some idea of how he'd be feelin. It was never just as simple as ye'd think. Not just who won or lost. It was how they played the game.

ALEC: **(saying it with her)** How they played the game.

MAE: It was one of the things he put his pride in. Ye know? He had a lot a pride.

JEANNIE: Yer soundin better, Ma.

MAE: Aye. I am, a bit. I feel like we're doin something positive.

JEANNIE: Well. Aye. I suppose. What was the best time, Ma? I mean. Was it when ye first met him, or what was it? I mean. I try to understand, but, we've no really talked about things very much before, I mean, about you and ma Da. There's still a lot of things I don't know about.

MAE: Ye mean sex?

JEANNIE: Ma . . .

MAE: I don't see what I'm supposed tae know about that you don't.

JEANNIE: I meant . . . were we ever happy?

She is on the edge of tears.

MAE: God aye, Jeannie. Course we were.

JEANNIE: Were we . . .

MAE: Aye, we were. There were always good things.

She stands.

MAE: There were always things we could be happy about.

She moves towards JEANNIE, but ALEC moves to her shoulder.

MAE: There still are, pet. I'm still glad that I've got you and Tam. Look. I feel like I want tae freshen masel up a bit. We'll have a proper talk later when we're feelin merr comfortable. Aye? Tell ye what. You come and help me get changed. Pick out somethin nice to wear.

JEANNIE: Don't ye want tae talk to me?

MAE: Jeannie. It's difficult.

JEANNIE: Why?

ALEC: Tell her.

MAE: It's always been difficult.

ALEC: Tell her the truth.

JEANNIE: Mum. What are ye so scared of? Are ye scared of me?

MAE: I'm scared for ye. I've been selfish. I should've been thinking about you . . .

ALEC: Uch, yer arse. Yer poison, ye've aye been poison. Look at her. Yer killin her.

MAE: Stop it.

JEANNIE: What?

MAE: I'm sorry, Jeannie. It'll have to wait till I'm myself again. Come and help me. I'm sorry.

JEANNIE: Okay. I suppose it's what I'm here for.

MAE exits. JEANNIE goes to whisky bottle. She pours and quickly drains a large glass. She exits.

Scene 12

TAM and DONALD enter on balcony above the main stage. TAM ushers DONALD towards the doorway into the house.

TAM: There ye go.

DONALD: I don't want tae push ye, son, but . . .

TAM: Donald. In.

DONALD goes in the doorway.

TAM: Dae yer best, son. Oh aye. Intae the valley of death. Don't forget yer mittens.

TAM goes in. DONALD enters stage below.

DONALD: Mae? Jeannie? Hello?

ALEC: Hello, Donald. What are you after. Comin courtin, maybe?

TAM enters stage below.

TAM: What's up?

DONALD: I dunno, son. Maybe something's happened.

TAM: They'll be up the stair. I'll check.

He goes to side.

TAM: Hello, it's me. **(To DONALD.)** That'll bring them runnin. **(He picks up the bottle.)** Who's been hittin this, then?

Enter JEANNIE.

JEANNIE: Hello, Thomas. Ye got Ma's message then.

TAM: Aye.

DONALD: How is she?

JEANNIE: She's fine.

TAM: I told him . . . Ma was mebbe not too well. I didnae see any harm in Donald knowin. Mebbe he can help.

JEANNIE: Ma's fine.

TAM: How are you?

JEANNIE: I'm managin. Just about. D'ye want some tea or anything. Something to eat?

TAM: I'm okay.

DONALD: Aye. I'm fine as well.

JEANNIE: We're all fine then. D'ye have a good afternoon.

TAM: Aye.

JEANNIE: We've been to the Barras.

TAM: Aye. Lizzie said ye phoned from there. Did ye get anythin nice?

JEANNIE: Forty two pounds and eighty pence.

TAM: What for?

JEANNIE: Well. Ma took the notion to sell off a few things we won't be needing any more.

TAM: I see. Just sort ae clearing things out.

JEANNIE: I think that's the idea.

TAM: I'm sorry, Jeannie. I'm sorry you don't . . . ye don't feel that ye can trust me.

JEANNIE: Any plans for tonight?

TAM: No plans. As far as I'm concerned, everythin's up for grabs. D'ye mind if I have a drink? D'ye want one?

JEANNIE: Aye. Okay.

TAM: Donald?

DONALD: Thanks, son.

As TAM pours, enter MAE.

MAE: Hello, everyone.

TAM gives JEANNIE the bottle and goes to his Mammie.

TAM: Oh, Ma. I'm sorry.

They hug.

DONALD: Hello, Mae. If it's not convenient . . . I just wanted tae see ye were all right.

MAE: Thanks, Donald. Take a seat. **(Pause. MAE looks at ALEC.)** Well, it's a full house, then. Where's Lizzie, Tam?

TAM: Aw, well she's gone on tae a party. I thought I might gie her a ring later on. But it's a pal of hers, ye know, and well, I think this is something for the MacSwineys, ye know.

JEANNIE: How's she getting on nowadays?

TAM: Uch. She's all right.

MAE: I like her. She used tae come and see us. When you were away. Some afternoons.

TAM: She said.

JEANNIE: Well, it's always been an open house that way. Hasn't it, Ma? Remember Donald, back in the Calton, Ma was a bit ae a legend. Aw the skinned wee knees used tae end up at our door. You'll mebbe no remember that, Tam?

TAM: Naw. No really.

JEANNIE: Because you had only just come along when we had to move. When Ma wasnae well after you were born.

DONALD: I remember that. Alec was awful worried for ye.

JEANNIE: Aye.

TAM: So that was when it all went wrong.

JEANNIE: How'd ye mean?

TAM: When I turned up.

MAE: Tam. That's enough.

TAM: That's what this is all about. Get it all out in the open.

DONALD: Now look Tam.

TAM: Ye never lived here, Donald. You don't know nothing.

MAE: I said that's enough. You've got a say, Tam, but ye don't have any right to talk that way about us. We're not here just to try and cut things into bits. We are here to try and find a way of getting on with each other, and if that's not your attitude then I don't think ye've anything to say.

TAM: That's what I want to do.

MAE: Good. Did Jeannie tell ye that we went tae the Barras the day?

TAM: Aye.

MAE: Did she tell ye why?

TAM: She said it was your idea.

MAE: Aye. We sold your father's things. We didn't get very much, but then we just had time to go to the one place. I wasn't very well this afternoon.

TAM: How d'ye mean, Ma?

MAE: Well. The first time was last night. I thought . . .

JEANNIE: Ma.

MAE: I want to talk about it.

TAM: Ye thought ye saw my Da. And ye thought ye saw him again this afternoon. Aw, Jesus.

MAE: Aye. And he's here now. There. Beside Jeannie. Now, unless you're all bein very clever, I know now that I'm the only one that sees him. And hears him.

DONALD: Ye mean . . . he talks tae ye? What does he say?

TAM: Jesus Christ, Donald?

MAE: What's wrong, son? Don't ye think it's a good question? He says aw kinds ae things. He says I murdered him. I lied tae him. I turned you against him. I betrayed him. And he says he loves Jeannie.

JEANNIE bursts into tears.

DONALD: What does he want, Mae?

MAE: I think he wants me dead.

JEANNIE: Stop it. Stop it. It's not ma Da. It's not ma Da. It's you. It's you.

MAE: Me what, Jeannie?

DONALD: Have ye spoken tae a priest.

MAE: I'll talk tae Father MacIlhenny. **(To JEANNIE.)** Tomorrow, Jeannie. When it gets that bad that you cannae help me. When my family cannae help me and my faith cannae help me and my friends cannae help me, then you think what you're thinking.

JEANNIE: How do you know what I'm thinking. I just think yer upset because my Dad died, my Da would never . . . yer not yersel.

63

MAE: It's not me that's not masel. It's him.

She points. TAM stares in ALEC's direction.

TAM: You leave me Ma alone.

ALEC: Fuckin make me.

ALEC gets up, and TAM is left to attack an empty chair.

MAE: Tam.

TAM: You old bastard. Ye sat on her yer whole life. Ye lied tae me and frightened her. Ye thought ye were a great man and ye were just a bitter old shite. Fuck off.

JEANNIE launches herself at him. MAE and DONALD try to separate them. ALEC steps forward towards the audience.

JEANNIE: You bastard.

ALEC: Pathetic. Nae fuckin discipline.

He sits. MAE holds JEANNIE. TAM stands with DONALD.

JEANNIE: You bastard.

ALEC: You tell him.

JEANNIE: Why did you come home?

TAM: I don't know. I don't know why.

JEANNIE: I've had enough. I'm not going to listen to all this.

MAE: Jeannie. I know ye loved yer Da. Yer Da know ye loved him. Ye don't have anything to prove.

JEANNIE: What about him? What's he trying to prove. I'm all right. I won't hit him. He's not worth it. Did you see him? Did ye?

TAM: No.

JEANNIE: Then what were you tryin to prove.

TAM: I hated him.

JEANNIE: I know you did. You've always hated everything decent.

TAM: You never loved him. You were just his fucking slave. You were fuckin married once, remember? But ye let yer Daddy break it up. What's wrong wi you. Everything decent? He wasnae decent. He was a feart wee nothin who tried tae be a monster. What does that make you?

MAE: You left me with her? Didn't ye. You were happy enough to go out gallivantin while I've been goin through aw this. You left Jeannie with me. Because you're feart, because you're pretending, because you are just like your Da. Yer just like him.

DONALD: Mae . . .

MAE: You let him push ye around, Donald. You let him do whatever he wanted. You weren't his friend you just followed him. And ye mooned around me. More than once, more than once, if you'd showed me some guts I'd have left him. But none of you gave me anywhere to go. At least, Tam, if yer Da was frightened, it's because he tried to face something, what he tried to believe was something worth believing. What are you trying to be? Jeannie's right. What do you think yer trying to prove.

TAM: Ma, he never gave me a chance, he told me I was nothing from the day I was born . . .

MAE: Are you saying he was right?

TAM: You helped him. You let him. I watched him treat ye like shite, I watched you takin it. I watched you watchin me takin it, and Donald takin it, and Jeannie takin it and lovin it, and you never tried tae stop him. It doesnae matter now. It doesnae matter.

The explosion is over. Pause. TAM sits down. Pause. ALEC walks slowly toward JEANNIE, circuitously.

MAE: Mebbe . . . mebbe we've all been let down. Eh? Mebbe we've all been disappointed.

DONALD: Mae. I mind somethin. Once. Fae a long time ago. Me and Alec. On Monte Cassino.

TAM: Oh, Christ, aye.

DONALD: You listen. Oh, me and yer Da told a lot of stories about that. But I never told ye this. Third night we were there. I was trying tae get some sleep. I was aw curled up intae ma helmet. Bunched up. Couldnae get comfortable, and I mind I woke up. And I saw yer Da. He was perched up on top ae the foxhole. Fearless. Shells screamin round him . . . bullets . . . he was smilin . . . he was conductin it. That's what I thought of. Conductin it like a band leader. Like Henry Hall or somebody. He was makin shells burst wi a movement of his hand. All around us. There was Glesga boys. Torn tae pieces. Turnin intae mud. And he felt . . . nae fellowship . . . at all. Nae danger. Nae pity. Nae fellowship at all. Yer right, Mae. I wasnae the man I might have been. I did follow him. Like ye say.

MAE: Donald . . .

DONALD: We brought a lot back wi us. From the war. Different things. But I was his friend. Have nae doubts on that. Mebbe he was a great man. But if he was, then there were thousands and thousands of great men, and he could never see that. I had my loyalty, Mae. If yer no a strong man, if what ye saw when you and yer pal went tae see the world, if that didnae leave ye stronger, if that just made ye think how . . . scared ye were, then loyalty's a lot. Ye know?

ALEC exits with JEANNIE. TAM gets up.

TAM: Ma. I said I'd phone Lizzie. Is it okay if I just nip doon the road. Just for a couple of minutes.

MAE: Aye. Okay.

TAM: I'm sorry we couldnae just sit down and be civilized. Ye know? Too much water under the bridge.

MAE: Mebbe. We still have to try, son. What'll ye tell her?

TAM: I dunno. Just thought I'd say hello.

MAE: Mebbe she'd like tae come over.

TAM: Ma. Nae party's that bad.

He exits.

MAE: See what ye've been missing, Donald. No having a family of yer own?

DONALD: Uch. I grew up in one. Is he still here?

MAE looks around. Pause.

MAE: Donald, where's Jeannie? **(She gets up.)** Jeannie. Oh, God, Donald. Where's Jeannie?

DONALD: I'll find her for ye.

She grabs his arm.

MAE: Don't leave me. We'll both look. Jeannie. Jeannie.

They exit. We hear them calling for her.

Scene 13

From this point on, all stage areas are used, with lighting changes to denote focus. The scenes, in real time, are simultaneous, and hence moments overlap and are repeated.

Loud music. Phone off the hook. LIZZIE enters. Picks it up.

LIZZIE: Hello, Tam? . . . Aye. . . . Sorry, sorry, it took Aileen a while tae find us. . . . Ye in a call box? . . . What? . . . **(She listens.)** Ye all right? . . . Of course I want tae talk tae ye. . . . I can't, Tam . . . no yet. . . . Aye, I know, we had the cops round. *I said we had the cops round.* . . . Aye, it was amazin. This guy Vinnie . . . did I tell ye about him? He got himsel stuck tryin tae crawl oot the bathroom window. . . . He was stoned oot his nut. . . . Naw, naw, Aileen's boyfriend went tae talk tae them. . . . Aye, he's a lawyer, they fucked right of. . . . What? Just the way he talked tae them, his accent . . . aye. Aye, I was goin oot the windae after Vinnie. . . . He's a dealer. . . . That the tones? . . . Have ye got? . . . What's your number? . . . Tam? . . . Say it again . . . 631 29 . . . what? . . . Aye I'll call ye back . . .what's the number? . . . Tam? Tam?

Silence, sudden, lights out on LIZZIE. Up on TAM putting phone down. Then back to LIZZIE. She considers for a moment, then decides. She speaks to someone at party.

LIZZIE: Scuse me? Scuse me . . . could ye shut that door a minute.

Lights down on LIZZIE, up on MAE and DONALD outside JEANNIE's room.

MAE: Jeannie? Ye in there ?

DONALD: Mebbe she just wants left alone.

MAE: He's in there with her. I know it. I know he is. Alec. Alec, you leave her alone. It's me ye want. Jeannie. Open the door.

DONALD: Mae . . .

JEANNIE: **(offstage)** Mum. Mum. I'm okay. I just want to be on my own for a minute, okay?

MAE: Jeannie, love. Ye okay?

JEANNIE: **(offstage)** Oh, ye know me, Mum. I'll be fine. Just leave me in peace for a minute. Eh?

DONALD: Come on, Mae.

MAE: He's in there.

DONALD: How d'ye know, Mae? Ye've no seen him. Did ye see him with her?

MAE: No, Donald, but . . .

DONALD: Mae. Ye've no seen him. Ye've no seen him. Mebbe he's gone. Mebbe Jeannie just needs a bit a time.

MAE: He's in there with her, he's in there with her.

DONALD: Mae, if Jeannie can't see him, what harm can he do, even if he is. Come on. *Come on*.

MAE: Donald . . . I killed him. He's right. In the hospital. Jeannie wouldnae let them turn off the machines. She kept waitin for some kinda miracle. She believed that miracles were the kinda thing that he deserved.

DONALD: Mae . . .

MAE: I switched him off . . . I waited till Jeannie was asleep and I let them switch him off. Donald, I didn't want him to wake up. God forgive me, I knew it in my heart, I didn't want him to get better. That's not him in there. It's me. It's my sin. It's my sin.

She breaks down. He holds her. We switch back to LIZZIE. Slowly, she puts the phone down. Then turns to go back to the party.

Scene 14

JEANNIE'S room. ALEC holds a mirror.

ALEC: That's it. Ye know now, don't ye? Yer standin alone, lassie. For decency. But ye know ye've got the angels on yer side.

JEANNIE: That's it. Int it, Jeannie. Ye know now. I cannae see it. I look okay. I'm bright. I do my best, don't I? I cannae see what's so wrong. Poor Jeannie, that's what they all say, poor, wasted, lonely old maid.

ALEC: Oh, there's nothin wrong wi you, darlin. That's the whole point. They despise ye for bein strong, for holdin up a mirror. It's themselves they don't like. Ye frighten them, that's aw.

MAE: **(offstage)** Jeannie, love, ye okay.

JEANNIE: Oh, ye know me, Mum. I'll be fine.

ALEC: They see a skull, their ain skull, and a wee worm a terror that crawls through the sockets, that bites them where they keep their secrets, it bites them, when they think the world's a bit too much.

JEANNIE: Just leave me alone for a minute, eh?

MAE: **(offstage)** He's in there with her, he's in there with her.

JEANNIE puts her hands over her ears.

ALEC: Wee snake bitin where they keep their dirty secrets, and it sends them mad.

Pause. JEANNIE waits until she thinks her mother's gone. She produces a bottle of whisky.

ALEC: See the thing to do? Relax. Naw, I mean it. You leave it aw tae me, pet. You've done what ye had tae.

JEANNIE: I cannae see it.

ALEC: Shoosh, noo. It's yer education. I know it's no easy.

JEANNIE: What is so wrong?

ALEC: Nothins wrong. Ye just have tae put yer loyalty where yer loyalty'll count. And ye've done that now.

JEANNIE: Couldnae haud on tae her man, ye know, aye, she even lost her Daddy.

ALEC: Mebbe ye shouldnae be drinking quite so fast, pet.

JEANNIE: Oh she copes so well with everything. She's such a wee treasure. Poor Jeannie. **(Furious.)** She's such a wee treasure.

ALEC: Jeannie . . .

TAM on balcony.

TAM: What did ye expect, eh? Be honest wi yersel. Ye'd just come home quietly and bury yer Daddy. Ye'd pick up yer love life from where ye left it off. Was that it? Right, well he's popped back up again, and yer love life's getting picked up at some party in the West End. So what ye gonnae dae? Yer gonnae get the money aff yer Ma, once she's no too busy seein ghosts, and yer gonnae get out. Just like they all expect ye to. Aye. And be honest wi yersel, that's what you expected. That's what you expected ye would do, give or take a detail, didn't ye? I mean ye try and hurt everybody first, of course. Got tae dae that. Oh aye, ye've got tae dae that and humiliate yersel as well if ye can manage. I meen ye've got a reputation here haven't ye? Yer gonnae run, aren't ye? Yer gonnae think. Yer no gonnae look, just so yer precious Tam can stay bein the kind a Tam he says he is. For ever and forever and forever. He kept himsel still and you kept yersel movin but ye both ended up right here. They're right, aren't they, Tam. You are. He's come back fae the grave, and you're gonna run away. Ye've got yer reputations. He's yer Da. And you're yer Daddy's boy.

MAE and DONALD outside JEANNIE's door.

JEANNIE: **(offstage)** She's such a wee treasure.

MAE: **(loudly to DONALD)** What was that?

DONALD: Mae. If she wants to be on her own.

MAE: She's not on her own, is she?

DONALD: I'm frightened for ye.

MAE: Ye mean it's him yer frightened of. Yer hero. What he's doin. What he's doin tae me.

DONALD: I'd nae idea about you. Ye hide bein angry. Much better than he ever did. If he was feart, and he couldnae show it, he couldnae admit it. Mebbe nor could you.

MAE: It was never safe, Donald. In this house. You couldnae show anybody anything. When I was ill. Efter I had Tam, things changed between me and Alec.

DONALD: Mae . . .

MAE: It turned intae a battle. He started forcin me every night, and somewhere deep down, he knew how I felt. And he hated it, and he hated me. And the bed was the place where he came tae take his vengence. Both ae us felt dirty, degraded, I suppose. And so disappointed. Because we knew we'd loved each other once, d'ye see. And the whole world went round and round and round us, the two ae us. At war in a bed. Donald, for all you ever felt frightened and alone, he felt it a hundred thousand times. So the rest ae us had tae feel it too. And it was never safe to say.

ALEC: **(offstage)** Mae . . . Mae . . . help me

MAE: I hear him.

ALEC: **(offstage)** Jeannie. Aw naw. Aw naw.

MAE beats at the door.

MAE: Donald, you'll have to help me.

Lights change. JEANNIE's room a few minutes earlier.

JEANNIE: What does it matter? What anybody thinks.

ALEC: That's right, that's right. The bastards, what dae they know?

JEANNIE: Whose fault. Ye knew already, didn't ye. It was gonnae be like this. Oh no the details. Ye were kiddin yersel.

ALEC: It's hard, I know it's hard.

JEANNIE: What else was anyone gonnae do? Tam was always gonnae come and then just bugger off, wasn't he?

ALEC: Aye. Aye.

JEANNIE: Maw was always gonnae kid herself that ma Daddy was a bastard and try and shove me out the way and it would aw fall tae bits and we'd all hate each other. That was always gonnae be the way of it.

ALEC: That's it, Jeannie. That's it. That's right. That's why you must be strong.

JEANNIE: An Jeannie. Jeannie was always gonnae be the one

73

tae pick up the pieces and put on a brave face, and show the world that his memory and his values still stood for something.

ALEC: That's it, Jeannie. That's it.

JEANNIE: There was nothing else for Jeannie, was there, that was it, that was always gonnae be the way. Jeannie had nothing else going for her? Did she?

ALEC: Jeannie . . .

JEANNIE: What was Jeannie gonnae do? Go out an get a lumber? Sing Halleluiah? Whit? Not our Jeannie. She was always gonnae do the decent thing. Well I cannae. I'm no up to it.

She takes pills from her pocket, pours them out.

ALEC: Jeannie don't.

JEANNIE: They pull at ye, Da? Don't they. Like ye said. Ye stand up, they smack ye doon. But if ye keep yer head doon, they still pull at ye and step on ye. Don't they. The family. The hoose. The neighbours, the work, the shopping, the hale scheme.

ALEC: Jeannie, stop it. Jeannie. This isnae what I wanted. Jeannie.

She starts to eat the pills. Washes them down with whisky.

JEANNIE: So ye have to be strong, don't ye, decent, principled, don't ye. What if yer not?

ALEC: Ye are. Ye are. *I tellt ye ye are*.

JEANNIE: See if yer no strong, or important, ye need tae make a deal, don't ye. Wi yersel, first. Ye tell yersel that if ye like yersel then ye can get out ae bed and do what ye dae next and that is ye make another deal wi where ye stay, wi yer hoose, and your close and yer street. Yer all gonnae like each other and get along nicely, then yer street makes a deal wi your postcode and yer postcode wi yer area and yer toon and your country and ye make nice wee deals aw the way tae the United fuckin Nations and Jesus Christ Almighty well it's just not happenin, Da, like ye said.

ALEC: Mae . . . Mae . . . help me . .

JEANNIE: It all went wrong, all ae it, all of the way from the stars up above tae ma face. Ma face there. I cannae see it. I cannae see ma face.

ALEC: Jeannie . . . please . . . I just wanted ye to be happy. I just wanted justice. I only wanted things tae be fair. **(He shakes her.)** Jeannie!

JEANNIE: **(waking, seeing him)** Daddy. *Dead. Dead.* **(Collapses.)**

ALEC: Jeannie . . . aw naw. Aw naw.

MAE: **(offstage)** Donald. Help me.

ALEC: You were gonnae rise above them. Jeannie. You were gonnae fly, Jeannie. **(MAE and DONALD come in.)** You murderin bitch.

MAE: What have you done?

ALEC: Ye satisfied, are ye? That you happy noo?

MAE: Donald. Phone for an ambulance. Donald.

ALEC: That the best that ye can do? Him?

MAE: The Johnstone's, Donald. Number 23.

ALEC: Look what you've done to her. Look what you've done.

MAE: Donald. Phone. Find Tam.

Exit DONALD.

ALEC: You've done it now, haven't ye. Ye've murdered me and ma Jeannie and now you and that traitor are gonnae laugh and laugh.

DONALD finds TAM on balcony.

DONALD: Tam.

TAM: What?

DONALD: Jeannie, she's tried tae kill hersel. In there, son, hurry.

DONALD and TAM exit from balcony.

ALEC: Get off her. Get off her.

MAE: She's not dead. Do ye want her dead? Do ye?

ALEC: What are ye daein tae her? What are ye daein?

MAE: How many did she take? Alec, how many did she take? Help me. Be her father. Help me.

TAM and DONALD enter JEANNIE'S room.

TAM: Ma what happened.

ALEC: You. Aye it's me you wee bastard. Ye'll burn in hell, baith of ye. Ye'll burn in hell. You're gonna pay. Ye'll baith die screamin. Ye'll baith die alone.

MAE: Tam.

TAM: He tried to kill her. He tried to kill Jeannie.

ALEC: Liar. Liar. I didnae.

TAM: You're not ma Da. Ma Da would never dae that. My Da died. Ma, ma, it's no my Da, it's not.

ALEC: I'm Alec MacSwiney.

TAM: You're not my Da. You're what killed him. You killed ma Dad.

ALEC: I'm Alec MacSwiney.

TAM: No. My father's dead. He was just a man, an ordinary man.

ALEC stares at them. And then at him. He exits, defeated. The living turn to each other over JEANNIE on the floor.

Scene 15

Graveside. Positions as at opening of scene one. MAE approaches the coffin.

MAE: Alec. I've been thinking of the night we first met. Ye caught me. Quick as that. I knew who ye were. Yer uniform. Yer shoulders. Yer wee tash. First dance. I mind ye walked me home. Miles and miles. And just at Clydebank, ye sat me on the wa o this bombed oot tenement, ye sat beside me. And ye told me yer dreams. You were gonnae change the world. You made me feel so brave. **(She sobs.)** I loved you, Alec. But ye were lost. Ye were lost. Losing you was hard. It seems like a long time ago.

Fade.

The End

The Breathing House

Peter Arnott

'As brothels and old-time religion nestle up in the back streets, auld reekie's well-heeled self image is chillingly blighted by death and disease. Obvious gothic antecedents here are Stevenson and Conan Doyle, but there are nods, too at David Lynch and Stanley Kubrick. In its brutal depiction of how sexual plague decimates societies great and small, however, it shows that even *Trainspotting's* darker roots go way back.'

Neil Cooper, The Herald

'The play's dramatic power comes from the passion with which it traces the story of two middle-class friends . . . this big, fast-moving filmic show unleases some rich, still topical arguments about class and sex, social reform, economics, Darwinian rationalism and religious fundamentalism, even the distant prospect of socialism.'

Joyce McMillan, The Scotsman

'Peter Arnott has cleverly given *The Breathing House* space for ensemble playing, with practically every role a star part in this *Upstairs Downstairs* world with a twist. It is a scenario that provides what must be one of the most incisive demolitions of so-called respectability ever seen on the boards.'

Kenneth Speirs, Scottish Daily Mail

ISBN 978-0-9551246-4-8

£6.99

Web orders at **www.fairplaypress.co.uk**

 Scottish **Arts** Council

Parking Lot in Pittsburgh
Anne Downie

'A piercing and funny look at how families control. Anne Downie's play rapidly transcends its own tight focus exposing us to wider issues and the abject hypocrisy of which we can all be guilty.

Moving, tender, tragic. Be prepared to laugh, weep and squirm!'

The Stage

'An appealing mixture of comedy and pathos that straddles continents as well as emotions. Intriguing that Anne Downie has taken individual notions of independence and co-dependence and used them as a metaphor for a country forever on the cusp. The extended routine on hormone replacement therapy is priceless!'

The Herald

'The strongest aspect of the writing lies in its treatment of the reality of emigration and the devastating accuracy of the relationships between the five sisters. Engaging human drama.'

The Guardian

ISBN 978-0-9551246-5-5

£6.99

Web orders at **www.fairplaypress.co.uk**

Scottish **Arts** Council

The White Bird Passes

Anne Downie

adapted from the novel by Jessie Kesson

'The most eye catching aspect of Downie's play is its capacity, recalling O'Casey, to portray the life of a colourful community. The work, which eschews facile sentimentality, gives voice to a wealth of striking characters and is a gripping and moving one.'

The Scotsman

'The sheer energy and purity of Kesson's vision, captured in Anne Downie's stage version, is irresistible. The story comes as a reminder that no human being has to be defined by what society calls disadvantage. *The White Bird* not only passes but soars!'

Scotland on Sunday

'Anne Downie's effective, faithful and ultimately heart-rending adaptation of Jessie Kesson's novel, a classic of Scottish literature . . . changes the perception that Scottish Theatre is about urban, usually Glasgow working class life and evokes a world just as vibrant and ruthless, where hardship and tragedy lie unmawkishly beside beauty and undauntable humanity.'

The Guardian

ISBN 978-0-9551246-7-9

£6.99

Web orders at **www.fairplaypress.co.uk**

 Scottish **Arts** Council

The Yellow on the Broom

Anne Downie

based on the novel by Betsy Whyte

'It can be no easy thing to find yourself, as travelling folk in Scotland long have, simultaneously the repository of conventional people's romanticism and the focus of their dark fears. It takes a real dramatist like Anne Downie, with her rich, enchanting and moving new play *The Yellow On The Broom* to give full expression to both aspects.

The lyrical lilt, the variety and vividness of character and scene make for memorable theatre.'

The Scotsman

'By turns heartwarming, painful, humorous and rousing. Above all it seems to grasp the essence of the travelling lifestyle. The play's ultimate form leaves one moved.'

The List

'A remarkable derivation by Anne Downie of Betsy Whyte's popular autobiography. The piece adroitly moves through time, using scenes, songs, and poetry to depict surprisingly interesting vignettes of everyday life on the road. A powerful memorial to the last days of the travelling people.'

Scotland on Sunday

ISBN 978-0-9551246-6-2

£6.99

Web orders at **www.fairplaypress.co.uk**

Scottish **Arts** Council